THE

ORIGIN AND RESULTS

OF THE

CLEARING SYSTEM,

WHICH IS IN OPERATION

ON THE

NARROW GAUGE RAILWAYS,

WITH TABLES

OF THE

THROUGH TRAFFIC IN THE YEAR 1845.

PRINTED BY SMITH AND EBBS, TOWER-HILL, LONDON.

1846.

In the interest of creating a more extensive selection of rare historical book reprints, we have chosen to reproduce this title even though it may possibly have occasional imperfections such as missing and blurred pages, missing text, poor pictures, markings, dark backgrounds and other reproduction issues beyond our control. Because this work is culturally important, we have made it available as a part of our commitment to protecting, preserving and promoting the world's literature. Thank you for your understanding.

THE ORIGIN AND RESULTS, &c.

The investigations which had their origin in the diversity of Gauge existing in this country, were the means of first introducing the Railway Clearing House to the notice of the public. Its existence was previously unknown except to persons in immediate connection with the Railway Companies, by which it had been established, and its real nature and objects are still very imperfectly understood beyond that circle.

It was stated, for example, in evidence, before the Gauge Commissioners, that "the "Clearing House system is simply a business-"like way of ascertaining where the carriages "are—It is a very business-like mode of "ascertaining the amount of stock that has run upon the different Lines, and balancing accounts as to that"*—"That there are frequent changes of passengers going by the different Lines, even on the Birmingham Line, at Rugby"—"That it is inevitable that for economy, convenience, and every other thing else, a change must be made there"—That "with regard to goods, it is as strikingly the case as with regard to passengers, that at those places wherever many " Lines converge, there must, to a great extent, be a re-assortment of goods"—That "it is the practice on existing Railways, at Birmingham for instance." †

As this evidence was given on very imperfect information by witnesses whose opinions on all subjects relating to Railways have deservedly great weight, it is deemed expe-

---

* Mr. Brunel's examination—Question 4033.

† Mr. Saunders' examination—Questions 3862, 3863, 3870, 3880, 3881.

dient to publish a concise account of the origin, objects, and extent of the Clearing arrangements, in order to remove the erroneous impressions which the statements, just quoted, are calculated to impart.

No sooner had the Railways which extend from London to Liverpool been completed and connected in 1838, than it became evident that arrangements must be adopted to facilitate the passage of the through traffic at the points where the three Railways joined. It was found that not only must passengers be permitted to perform any journey within the limits to which continuous communication by Railway extended, without being required to change their carriage, but that a similar principle must pervade the arrangements for working every description of through traffic if the public were to be conciliated, and the resources of the Railway system developed to their full extent.

The expediency of taking this course in

relation to the through traffic became still more evident at a subsequent period, when the chain of Railways, which connect the metropolis and York, was opened throughout.

On both occasions, the Directors of the respective Railways yielded to the necessities of their position; and endeavoured to comply with the wishes of the public as far as the incomplete state of the works at the opening of the Lines permitted, and thus originated what has been since termed the Clearing System.

The system in the simple form in which it was first reduced to practice, produced unforeseen results, the tendency of which was to create dissensions between the Companies, and to prove injurious to their interests.

In the first place, the methods of keeping accounts adopted by the several Railway Companies were in no two cases exactly similar;

and this diversity of system caused much difficulty and confusion when the accounts came to be compared for the purpose of effecting a settlement. Long delays occurred, and much angry correspondence, not unfrequently passed between the Managers, before payment of the sums due by one Company to the other, could be obtained. In the next place, although all the connected Companies had entered into an agreement to render accurate returns of the use they respectively made of one another's carriages and waggons, and to pay a fixed rate per mile, for whatever distance they ran—still the conditions of the agreement, were from the first, very imperfectly fulfilled, and some of the Companies came in the end to make an unacknowledged use of the carriages and waggons of others to an extent which amounted to a positive grievance.

It was while the measures best adapted for obviating these admitted evils were under consideration, that it occurred, about the same time, to Mr. Robert Stephenson and the present Manager of the Railway Clearing House, that a Central Office constituted on the principle of the City Clearing House would furnish the remedy sought. When the idea was suggested to Mr. Glyn, he saw, at a glance, its practical bearing, lent the whole weight of his great influence to procure its being realized in practice, and was mainly instrumental in accomplishing that object.

Mr. Hudson likewise gave the proposed establishment his powerful support; and both Mr. Creed and Capt. Laws entered warmly into the plan, and took an active part in removing the objections which the superior officers of some of the Railways at first entertained to the system.

But, notwithstanding the influence and efforts of the gentlemen just named, a considerable period elapsed before every obstacle was removed, and every arrangement completed.

Finally, however, on the 2nd January, 1842, the system of the Railway Clearing House came into operation on the Railways extending from London to Darlington in one direction, and from Manchester to Hull in another. It was adopted at subsequent periods by the Companies whose Railways extend from Darlington to Carlisle, Sunderland, Hartlepool, and Scarborough; and from Birmingham to Gloucester, Birkenhead, Liverpool, Fleetwood, Lancaster and Manchester And in a few months it will be in force on all the Railways included in the area defined by a Line passing from London through Gloucester, Liverpool, Fleetwood, and Glasgow, to Edinburgh;—and returning by Berwick, Newcastle, Scarborough, Hull, Yarmouth, and Cambridge, to the Metropolis, or in other words on all the narrow gauge Railways in Great Britain lying North of the Thames, with the exception of the few short Lines which are beyond the limits of the area just described.

The main principles of the system thus widely diffused, are, *first*, that passengers shall be booked through at all principal stations, and conveyed to their destination without change of carriage;—that horses and cattle shall likewise be sent through without change of conveyance, and that goods shall, in the same way, be carried through without being either shifted or re-assorted. *Secondly*, that the Companies respectively shall pay a fixed rate per mile, for such carriages and waggons not their own property, as they may use; and a further sum per day by way of fine or demurrage for detention, if kept beyond a prescribed length of time: and, *lastly*, that no direct settlement shall take place between the Companies in respect of any traffic, the accounts of which have passed through the Railway Clearing House.

These are the fundamental principles of the Clearing system, and though the regulations based on them are occasionally deviated from, the portion of traffic subjected to such deviation is insignificant when compared with the immense extent of the traffic in relation to which the regulations are strictly observed. That these regulations are departed from at all, is the result less of necessity than of defective arrangements which invariably disappear when the traffic reaches a point that compels the application of a remedy. The re-arrangement of trains, which in the evidence already referred to, is represented as indispensable at the points at which Railways converge, is never adopted in practice; on the contrary, the main design of the Clearing arrangements is to prevent recourse being had to a plan which, as is well known to practical men, would act as a serious impediment, and cause great delay and confusion. It is true that re-assortment of goods does take place to a limited extent at one or two points of convergence; but at the greater number of such places such an operation is never known to occur, and never will occur to any extent, because the expense, the loss of time, and the damage to the load which it necessarily involves, will prevent its being resorted to, if it can by possibility be avoided. In short, the tendency of the Clearing arrangements is, and judging from what they have already accomplished, their ultimate result will be, to give to all the connected Railways of Great Britain, as far as regards the working of the through traffic, the character of one concern, conducted on a uniform system, the chief aim of the system being to prevent delay or disturbance of the load during the journey.

The portion of the Clearing system which relates to the settlement of accounts, consists of arrangements, which are simple in character, and capable of unlimited extension. From each of the Clearing House Stations there are sent daily to the Central Office in London:—

1. A return of the passengers booked through.
2. A return of the horses, private carriages, and cattle booked through.
3. A return of the parcels booked through.
4. A return of all the carriages, waggons, &c., which have arrived or been dispatched, either loaded or empty.

Along with these returns are sent all the through tickets collected, and all the parcels' way-bills received during the day.

From the returns thus transmitted, after they have been examined, compared, and analyzed, other returns are drawn up in the Railway Clearing House, and forwarded to the respective Companies in a form which admits of their being verified by the parties receiving them, and exhibiting in detail the portion of the receipts of the through traffic to which each Company is entitled, and the liabilities it has incurred by using the carriages and waggons of others.

The final settlement of the accounts is effected by the Railway Clearing House paying, or receiving the balances as the case may be, through the hands of the bankers who act as agents in London to the several Companies. In this way all the transactions of one Company, with all the other Companies, amounting frequently to many thousand pounds per week, are cleared weekly, by the remittance of a sum seldom exceeding a few hundred pounds.

The Railway Clearing House is under the control of a Committee, composed of the Chairmen of all the Railway Companies who are parties to the Clearing arrangements. The Committee holds two General Meetings in the course of the year, and Special Meetings as often as there may be occasion. The resolutions of the Committee are passed in the form of recommendations to the Companies, to adopt the measures proposed, and have no force until they obtain the confirmation of the respective Boards of Directors.

The expense of maintaining the Establishment is divided rateably among the Companies, in the ratio of the extent of business transacted for each, after a fixed sum has been first carried to the debit of each Company, for each of its stations, from which accounts are sent to the Clearing House.

It will not be out of place here to notice a few of the more remarkable effects which have proceeded from the Clearing system since the Railway Clearing House was instituted, and to advert to some objects not yet included in its arrangements, but for which it may be made available.

Reference was made in the foregoing part of these observations to the difficulties which, in the first stage of the Clearing system, retarded the settlement of the accounts of the through traffic, and to the asperities which found their way into the correspondence of parties, each of whom believed himself right, and whose pecuniary interests might possibly be affected by a contrary admission. This fruitful source of dissension and ill-will has been removed, and whatever slight differences do now occasionally arise, are adjusted without difficulty by the intervention of the Railway Clearing House. Allusion was also made to the practice of making an extensive use of carriages and waggons without acknowledgment, which had grown into a serious evil. The means which are possessed in the Railway Clearing House, of tracing each vehicle from the moment it leaves the parent Line until it returns to it, and of obtaining payment of the sums in which the Railway Companies become reciprocally indebted under the regulations of mileage and demurrage, soon checked, and has now put a complete stop to this practice. Further, the large sums which many of the Companies found themselves under the necessity of paying when these regulations came to be strictly enforced, induced them to add to the number of the Railway vehicles which they previously possessed. The larger number of the Companies on whose Lines the Clearing system is in operation, have now a sufficient number of the various kinds of conveyances required for working Railway traffic; and those Companies whose stock is still inadequate to their wants, are rapidly supplying the deficiency. The value of the large accumulation on the connected Railways, of carriages, waggons, and other vehicles, which thus resulted from the Clearing arrangements, was fully appreciated last year, when the great augmentation of nearly every description of through traffic, which rapidly took place, would have seriously embarrassed the executive departments of the several Companies, had they not, as regards their carrying stock, been so well prepared.

In estimating the advantage of the system under consideration, it would be a great oversight if no notice were taken of the beneficial results which flow from the occasional meetings of gentlemen whose position at their respective boards is the best proof of their influence. At these meetings there is generally present a number of the superior officers of the several Companies. The large amount of practical knowledge which is thus brought to the discussion of whatever questions may be under review, and the opportunities of mutual explanations which are afforded, have often the very best effects, in clearing up misconceptions, in reconciling differences, and in leading to the adoption of measures which have frequently an important bearing on the interests both of the Railway body and of the public.

But the great, the crowning achievement of the Clearing system is the facility, the economy, and the expedition with which it enables the Railway Companies to work the through traffic. The exceptional cases in which the Clearing regulations are infringed, demonstrate more clearly their value and importance, for whenever such infringement takes place, public dissatisfaction is excited, and the development of the traffic is checked. One needs but to reflect on the incalculable benefits which the proprietors of great undertakings derive from concentration of management and unity of system, to be convinced of the utility of an institution, the object and tendency of which is, to promote and establish uniformity of arrangements on the great net-work of British Railways, and to impose a check on the disposition to introduce diversities of system, which from some motive or other the managers of Railways have not unfrequently evinced.—In fact the advantages of the Clearing system, in relation to the influence which Railways exert on all the great national interests, cannot be overestimated. It had its origin, as has been shown, in the desire of Railway Companies to promote their own interests, in the only way in which they can be effectually promoted, or placed in a position of permanent security; that is, by consulting public opinion. It has grown with the growth of the Railway system,—and unless the public accommodation be restricted, and the exigencies of the commercial, manufacturing, and agricultural interests disregarded, it must advance to the limits to which continuous communication by Railway extends.

It will suffice to advert briefly to the objects not yet included in the Clearing arrangements, for which they may be made available.

By a simple and inexpensive plan they may be applied to the recovery and restoration of lost luggage. According to the proposed plan, the owner of luggage, lost within the limits to which the Clearing System reaches, would have simply to apply to the Central Office in London, where his instructions would be taken as to the mode of returning the luggage if found; or from which inquiries would be addressed to the proper parties with the view of tracing it, if it had not been previously reported.

Hitherto the accounts of the through traffic

in goods have not been passed through the Railway Clearing House, because the traffic is almost entirely in the hands of the established carriers, who settle their accounts with each Company separately and directly. But when the period arrives, and it is believed to be rapidly approaching, when all Railway Companies will themselves become carriers of goods, and when an uniform scale of charges will have been adopted throughout the kingdom; then these accounts may be subjected to the process of examination and adjustment pursued in the Railway Clearing House, with as great ease and regularity as any other division of Railway accounts.

The reader may remember, it was stated that the portion of the Clearing arrangements which relates to the settlement of accounts, may be expanded indefinitely. So true is this, that passengers may, when the opportunity offers, be booked through, not only between all the towns in the United Kingdom, which may possess the advantages of communication by Railway, but between those towns, and all the larger towns on the Continent, which may be equally fortunate, the Railway Clearing House being in both cases the medium of communication between Companies, and the channel through which a settlement of accounts will be effected.

Another most important purpose for which the Clearing arrangements may be more extensively used than they are at present, is the collection and arrangement of statistical information on all the points in the Railway system regarding which it is of moment that such information should exist in an authentic form.

Finally, it has been suggested that the principle of centralization involved in the Clearing arrangements, might be extended with advantage to matters bearing exclusively on the private interests of Railway Companies, such as the supply of carrying stock; but this is a question too large and complex to enter on here, especially as such a course would in no way promote the design with which this brief account of the Clearing system is presented to the public.

In conclusion, it remains to invite attention to the Tables of the Through Traffic, in 1845, which are annexed. These tables furnish the best refutation of the evidence which led to the publication of the foregoing remarks.

It will be found on reference to the Tables, that in the year named, 517,888 passengers were each conveyed through an average distance of 146 miles. That the average length of the Railways on which the Clearing system is in operation, is 41 miles; and that consequently, each passenger travelled over nearly four Railways on the average, and must have passed three junctions or points of convergence. To accommodate these passengers, 59,765 Railway carriages, and 5,813 trucks with private and whose pecuniary interests might possibly be affected by a contrary admission. This fruitful source of dissension and ill-will has been removed, and whatever slight differences do now occasionally arise, are adjusted without difficulty by the intervention of the Railway Clearing House. Allusion was also made to the practice of making an extensive use of carriages and waggons without acknowledgment, which had grown into a serious evil. The means which are possessed in the Railway Clearing House, of tracing each vehicle from the moment it leaves the parent Line until it returns to it, and of obtaining payment of the sums in which the Railway Companies become reciprocally indebted under the regulations of mileage and demurrage, soon checked, and has now put a complete stop to this practice. Further, the large sums which many of the Companies found themselves under the necessity of paying when these regulations came to be strictly enforced, induced them to add to the number of the Railway vehicles which they previously possessed. The larger number of the Companies on whose Lines the Clearing system is in operation, have now a sufficient number of the various kinds of conveyances required for working Railway traffic; and those Companies whose stock is still inadequate to their wants, are rapidly supplying the deficiency. The value of the large accumulation on the connected Railways, of carriages, waggons, and other vehicles, which thus resulted from the Clearing arrangements, was fully appreciated last year, when the great augmentation of nearly every description of through traffic, which rapidly took place, would have seriously embarrassed the executive departments of the several Companies, had they not, as regards their carrying stock, been so well prepared.

In estimating the advantage of the system under consideration, it would be a great oversight if no notice were taken of the beneficial results which flow from the occasional meetings of gentlemen whose position at their respective boards is the best proof of their influence. At these meetings there is generally present a number of the superior officers of the several Companies. The large amount of practical knowledge which is thus brought to the discussion of whatever questions may be under review, and the opportunities of mutual explanations which are afforded, have often the very best effects, in clearing up misconceptions, in reconciling differences, and in leading to the adoption of measures which have frequently an important bearing on the interests both of the Railway body and of the public.

But the great, the crowning achievement of the Clearing system is the facility, the economy, and the expedition with which it enables the Railway Companies to work the through traffic. The exceptional cases in which the Clearing regulations are infringed, demonstrate more clearly their value and importance, for whenever such infringement takes place, public dissatisfaction is excited, and the development of the traffic is checked. One needs but to reflect on the incalculable benefits which the proprietors of great undertakings derive from concentration of management and unity of system, to be convinced of the utility of an institution, the object and tendency of which is, to promote and establish uniformity of arrangements on the great net-work of British Railways, and to impose a check on the disposition to introduce diversities of system, which from some motive or other the managers of Railways have not unfrequently evinced.—In fact the advantages of the Clearing system, in relation to the influence which Railways exert on all the great national interests, cannot be overestimated. It had its origin, as has been shown, in the desire of Railway Companies to promote their own interests, in the only way in which they can be effectually promoted, or placed in a position of permanent security; that is, by consulting public opinion. It has grown with the growth of the Railway system,—and unless the public accommodation be restricted, and the exigencies of the commercial, manufacturing, and agricultural interests disregarded, it must advance to the limits to which continuous communication by Railway extends.

It will suffice to advert briefly to the objects not yet included in the Clearing arrangements, for which they may be made available.

By a simple and inexpensive plan they may be applied to the recovery and restoration of lost luggage. According to the proposed plan, the owner of luggage, lost within the limits to which the Clearing System reaches, would have simply to apply to the Central Office in London, where his instructions would be taken as to the mode of returning the luggage if found; or from which inquiries would be addressed to the proper parties with the view of tracing it, if it had not been previously reported.

Hitherto the accounts of the through traffic

in goods have not been passed through the Railway Clearing House, because the traffic is almost entirely in the hands of the established carriers, who settle their accounts with each Company separately and directly. But when the period arrives, and it is believed to be rapidly approaching, when all Railway Companies will themselves become carriers of goods, and when an uniform scale of charges will have been adopted throughout the kingdom; then these accounts may be subjected to the process of examination and adjustment pursued in the Railway Clearing House, with as great ease and regularity as any other division of Railway accounts.

The reader may remember, it was stated that the portion of the Clearing arrangements which relates to the settlement of accounts, may be expanded indefinitely. So true is this, that passengers may, when the opportunity offers, be booked through, not only between all the towns in the United Kingdom, which may possess the advantages of communication by Railway, but between those towns, and all the larger towns on the Continent, which may be equally fortunate, the Railway Clearing House being in both cases the medium of communication between Companies, and the channel through which a settlement of accounts will be effected.

Another most important purpose for which the Clearing arrangements may be more extensively used than they are at present, is the collection and arrangement of statistical information on all the points in the Railway system regarding which it is of moment that such information should exist in an authentic form.

Finally, it has been suggested that the principle of centralization involved in the Clearing arrangements, might be extended with advantage to matters bearing exclusively on the private interests of Railway Companies, such as the supply of carrying stock; but this is a question too large and complex to enter on here, especially as such a course would in no way promote the design with which this brief account of the Clearing system is presented to the public.

In conclusion, it remains to invite attention to the Tables of the Through Traffic, in 1845, which are annexed. These tables furnish the best refutation of the evidence which led to the publication of the foregoing remarks.

It will be found on reference to the Tables, that in the year named, 517,888 passengers were each conveyed through an average distance of 146 miles. That the average length of the Railways on which the Clearing system is in operation, is 41 miles; and that consequently, each passenger travelled over nearly four Railways on the average, and must have passed three junctions or points of convergence. To accommodate these passengers, 59,765 Railway carriages, and 5,813 trucks with private carriages, were sent through. It further appears, that 180,606 waggons, loaded with merchandize, were sent through, in addition to the large number of waggons used for the conveyance of coke, coal, and other minerals, of which no record is kept in the Railway Clearing House.

These striking facts will enable the reader to form an adequate conception of the present magnitude of the Through Traffic, and of the degree of accommodation which is given to the various classes of the community, and to all the great national interests. Further, they cannot fail to impress deeply on the public mind, the grave evils which must inevitably result from any cause tending to impede or interrupt the transit of a traffic, which, large as it is, can only be considered as a fraction of the extent to which the traffic of future years will attain.

A Return of the Number of Passengers Booked through on the Railways with which the Railway Clearing House is connected, in the year 1845.

NAME OF COMPANY.	1st Class.	2nd Class.	3rd Class.	Total number of Passengers Booked through.	Number of Miles Travelled by Passengers Booked through.
London and Birmingham...	83,199	61,728	19,992	164,919	31,009,298
Midland........................	36,143	45,154	5,590	86,887	10,610,614
Manchester and Leeds......	8,898	15,781	4,501	29,180	2,250,972
York and North Midland...	19,671	28,116	9,790	57,577	5,960,615
Great North of England...	7,350	9,370	8,223	24,943	2,508,087
Newcastle and Darlington..	14,269	21,250	7,728	43,247	5,567,045
Stockton and Darlington...	753	1,264	167	2,184	150,265
Stockton and Hartlepool...	2,863	7,467	2,080	12,410	449,278
Newcastle and Carlisle......	493	304	—	797	142,862
Birmingham and Gloucester	3,931	3,290	—	7,221	921,420
Manchester & Birmingham	10,698	1,876	450	13,024	2,998,673
Grand Junction	34,799	12,708	9,452	56,959	10,425,925
Chester and Birkenhead ...	2,440	1,010	—	3,450	553,428
North Union	2,595	3,001	608	6,204	628,976
Lancaster and Preston......	4,387	1,636	—	6,023	1,029,864
Preston and Wyre	1,521	1,342	—	2,863	575,827
Total......	234,010	215,297	68,581	517,888	75,783,149

Average Mileage of each Passenger, - - - - 146 Miles.
Average Length of the Railways connected with the Clearing-House, 41 ,,
Average Number of Junctions passed by each Passenger, - - 3·61